i

I doubted that this would reach your eyes. Doubted that I could string the words together into sentences, and in turn that these sentences could become passages that one might follow or consider as a sequential journey through the pages. The truth is: I had lacked the confidence. Lacked the belief required to achieve this imagined structure (whatever it could be). I would only wander so far through the process before my mental strength waned, the words drifting off on their scraps of paper, grammatical islands that found themselves conveniently hidden in cardboard boxes or on bookshelves, perpetually out of reach. I questioned the reasons for this lack of persistence, proposed that I required an adequate restriction, a limitation that could set a strong trajectory to plough through the doubt; that would enable me to follow the words to their unknown destination. I had begun to attach a sense of shame to this inability, desperately searching for a pragmatic solution to this invisible outline. The imagined object seemed too perfect. There was no reality, no printed paper scent, only the smell of the surrounding room: the intermingling of damp washing and a recently poached egg. Unpleasant. How could I negotiate the many directions on offer? What fragments deserved to be saved from the avalanche of time? The washing would need to be packed once dry, the burnt residue scoured from the frying pan. It would be polite to leave the house in a good condition, especially with my impending absence.

There. A restriction appears. It becomes a fact, my body cooped inside this moving space. A space I cannot leave without the risk of serious injury, propelled on wheels at a high speed, most probably seventy miles an hour based on my knowledge of motorway speed restrictions. I, *myself*, am horizontal. Laid out flat on my back in a bunk. I imagine an exploded view of the vehicle, in which the cladding and components are stripped away from around me. I hover above the conveyor of tarmac, dressed only in makeshift pyjamas consisting of a cotton t-shirt and synthetic football shorts. It is an odd image I agree, the scene transforming with this thought, rendering itself as a child's drawing, lines scribbled in colouring pens, ones with lids that have been chewed.

I choose to pick up the book beside me in the bunk, the one placed like a tent on the duvet, its entrance acting as the temporary marker for the page I have reached. Upon lifting the pages closer to my eyes, I cast myself back into the memory of previous readings. Despite my prior knowledge of the textual landscape, my new context offers an association between myself and the protagonist — also the writer. He is similarly restricted in the space that he has designated himself. His position is, however, less of a hover, and more of an oscillation. He floats on a liquid, mimicking the movements of the waves below him. The writing, rather scrupulously, describes the effects of this motion on his actions, often forcing him to leave his bunked position to make an urgent dash to the boat's bathroom. I begin to hope that his sickness does not become another shared association between us and, in the paranoia of this thought, I plan my own route to the small on-board toilet, which would involve stumbling through the pitch-black aisle between numerous sleeping bodies. I would be embarrassed to wake them in this event, especially to the sound of retching or — even worse — the sound's resulting mess.

His bodily restriction was self-imposed: he had asked for permission to board the vessel with the hope that the isolation might offer him the impetus for a novel. My written action was more of a consequence, an attempt to make the most out of the dead hours of travelling, periods of time that I usually wasted trying to visualise the future events that the destination would offer. There would be many of these moments on this journey, and despite the secondary movement enforced by the bus, my limbs would be stuck, stationary, the lack of physical exertion no doubt encouraging the mind's wander.

iii

My association to the seasick writer
becomes more literal than I had
expected, whilst once again, laying
in the bunk. A black box measuring
roughly seven by three feet, with small,
draw-back curtains to block out the
light. The walls are lined with hard
wearing black fabric, not the luxurious
silk of a coffin, but the type that you
would more likely associate with a car
boot. This limited interior includes a
netted pocket to hold personal items,
threads strung through a moulded
plastic frame and screwed into the
ceiling above my face. I had already
tested its capabilities, the tube of
toothpaste (so essential to this journey)
slipping through the gauze to land
on my eye whilst I drifted off in the
darkness. The next interruption came
in the early hours, and had been the
reason for the further association, my
eyes opening to the sound of waves
crashing, my body able to feel the
rise and fall through the mattress
that cradled my spine. I had begun to
become well acquainted with the back-
and-forth motion of the vehicle's hum,
but these forces came as a surprise.
They rocked the box inconsistently
from side to side and were followed by
a natural crescendo, audible through
the dampened walls. I couldn't help but
imagine the depths beneath, especially
in the deficit of light. If the boat
went down, we would be completely
unaware, the next interruption being a
cascade of water crashing down the
aisle before it engulfed the bunks and
their connected corpses. I spend a
short time thinking that I should have
woken and exited the car deck, but I'm
too tired to move. The promise of sleep
is worth more than the risk assessment.
I squeeze the soft contents of the
toothpaste tube in an attempt to forget
the movements below.

iv

The vehicle's tinted windows prevent
chronology. It becomes impossible to
estimate the time of day without the
aid of a device. The first minutes that
follow an uncomfortable manoeuvre
from the bunk become a guessing
game, based upon the hours that I
feel I have managed to sleep. Each
(probable) morning, having descending
the staircase, I am offered a limited
view from a filtered window. This
becomes the painted portrait of each
location, the first introduction to its
geography, no matter how accurate or
misleading. Today's painting is a flat
canvas coated with a crust of graffiti, a
layer of faceless words that will not be
deciphered, no matter how hard I will
try. I continue to be duped into believing
this reproduction held in its frame. The
illusion only broken when a limping
homeless man drags a trolley across
its surface. His face is another painting
that I cannot read.

v

I sit on the step of the vehicle, the one
that is revealed by the click of a plastic
switch — the type that springs back
into its dormant position following its
activation. The switch's use is shortly
followed by a hydraulic hiss, the door
swinging open to offer the view of
the morning, natural light flooding the
tinted darkness of the interior. The
view from the step is a particularly
unremarkable one: a tarmac loading
compound flanked by a fence framing
a weed-covered verge and a distinctly
grey sky that matches a concrete train
line running above. The props and
characters of this scene are scarce:
a solitary magpie wanders, looking
for a glint in the dirt, a lorry's trailer
sits stationary in satisfying geometry.
On closer inspection, the trailer's
markings do not discern its function,
but its weathered surface does offer
some evidence of a past use. Subtle
differentiations gradually appear in
this filthy layer, and my eyes are able
to construct a logo, a shape that was
once there but had since been
removed, a history explained in an
archive of gunk. It is still too abstract
though, there is simply no possibility for
the assemblage of meaning, but this
deficit encourages my own proposal
of function, my imagination forced to
bestow a connotation on the scene. The
image becomes a symbol, becomes a
reminder of the treacherous journeys
that many execute in search of an
improved future. The unremarkable
details are transformed in that moment,
disappearing behind the hiss of
the switch.

vi

I knew the maze of paths and I knew each gate,
The rose gardens and the graffiti-ed stage.
It was this familiarity that filled me with sadness, and it hung over,
matched the foggy grey.

I pretended to enjoy the scene, pointing out falling leaves,
but all along I felt like leaving.
After all, I knew the gates, could have done so easily.

Instead I found refuge, in a cafe, thought a poorly pronounced coffee could stave
off the memory.
And with limited success, charged my phone, at the opportunity,
an intriguing locker system that cost one euro fifty.

I returned to my seat and stared wistful, as bikes passed, like we used to.
How long should I wait for my money's worth, even in piles of autumnal dirt.
But surely the battery's charged to green, enabling me to navigate streets.

And so, agitated, I return to the machine.
But the card won't register,
I tap wildly on the screen:
Perhaps this is purgatory,
Perhaps I'll never leave?

I did not sleep well, remembering the sensation of each bump and curve in the road, the resulting vibrations preventing the flawless dreams of the night. This was not helped by my bladder which, by now, was bursting full, forcing me upright from the bunk and into the pitch-black. I skitter urgently down the dark aisle past snoring bodies, navigating blindly by hand, towards a crack of daylight that leaks up the vehicle's stairs. Despite the inconvenience the relief is an immense pay-off, even more so when I direct the off-yellow trickle into the very centre of the aperture: satisfaction as the dull stinging throb disappears with an audible sigh. The sigh punctuates my train of thought, prompts me of the tasks of the forthcoming day, reminding me that I must first receive an important parcel, scheduled to be delivered to the neighbouring theatre. There would be no other chance, the vehicle shortly rolling on to its next destination. These logistics are quickly distracted by the presence of sight, noticing a man in the vehicle's window frame as I exit the toilet. He wears a brown shirt and matching trousers, there is something visibly odd to his clashing choice of outfit, somewhat outdated in context, marking him as a misfit of the street. Furthermore, his body language suggests some kind of confusion, it is written clearly on his face as he passes once more.

My sleepless brain suddenly accelerates, to be followed shortly by my legs. A connection between colour and expression has finally formed, albeit inconveniently slowly. I sprint up the staircase, repeat the stumble through the aisle and wrestle on yesterday's jeans and t-shirt. The shade of his disappearing image now comfortably matching the branding of a particular global delivery company.

The door hisses at the command of the switch, revealing the yellow sting of daylight, and then I am out in the world. In pursuit. In the middle of the road with bare feet, my soles recoiling from the roughness of the tarmac. I am forced to change tack as he wanders into the distance, surely my voice would be able to cover the ground more efficiently, but would he think I was homeless? Would he think I was inciting an act of aggression? I volley words at his faceless back. He turns, his face now clear, offering a language I can't understand. Then he gives up in annoyance, in response to my lack of response, falls back on his limbs, his outstretched finger pointing to the façade of a cafe across the street, a cardboard box sitting in the window.

Further relief.

viii

After the activity of the evening dies, the theatre lights are switched on like an x-ray. The romance is stripped back and the bare bones are revealed. You could comb through the flotsam if you wanted to, perhaps finding an expensive item of clothing or a desirable sum of currency amongst the broken bottles. I, *myself*, am left with a solitary artefact: a t-shirt, its sweat-sodden cotton usually safely stowed away in the corner of a backstage room. I search for a modest container to house this unwanted relic, must prevent its saturation from seeping into the other items in my bag. After all, I would not want the pages of my notebook to stick together, would not want this text to bleed. Last night, I found the discarded wrapping from a multipack of water bottles, but tonight I steal a flush-cut document wallet from the theatre's production office. The t-shirt slots in perfectly, in a satisfying disregard of its corporate function.

ix

We eat dinner on the dancefloor, a
candle-lit table set to perfection in the
centre of a parquet maze, looking more
like a theatre set than a habitual choice
within its context. The thought is no
doubt encouraged by the surrounding
architecture: a repurposed 1930's
cinema, complete with sweeping,
up-lit balconies and plush, red folding
seats, the building gradually sloping
towards the now-absent screen. This
meticulous set gives me a sense of
unease, appearing as a contradiction
to the impending event in which I
will participate. The table — like the
silence and the screen — would shortly
disappear, to be replaced by the swell
of unsteady feet. My unease comes
from my mind's attempt to prepare the
body for its role in this spatial change. I
must spoil the ambient perfection of the
scene, must ruin it with the movements
of my flashing limbs.

If the moment was transformed into the silver screen of cinema, then the seamlessness of scene would be interrupted by an incongruous detail. Something that sticks out like a sore-thumb, the placement of an object or sound that belongs to another world. This detail would persist until the character (in this case *me*) becomes too aware to ignore it, summoned into its erroneous allure. It is at this startling point that the shot would cut, revealing that the previous scene was in fact an illusion, a dreamscape, the new shot presenting the character visibly shaken from the pillow. This is the state in which I find myself: thuds and vibrations have penetrated the dream, significant enough to have travelled through the chassis of the stationary vehicle. Despite a lack of evidence I am confident that it is the middle of the night and my mind begins to grasp for explanations for the commotion. Perhaps it was a gang who had taken exception to the size and grandeur of the vehicle, perhaps extremists who had taken offence to the liberal emphasis of the evening's performance. The anxiety is quelled by a shout, bodies race out of the bunks around me, and I crane my neck between the curtains, flashes of skin appear in the darkness, legs hopping and twisting into pairs of jeans before charging down the stairs. I am slow to react, and recognise that in the spirit of camaraderie I should follow suit, but as soon as I am partially clothed I realise I've missed the moment, and the unseen event has already diffused. It seems that I had remained in the dream for too long but at least the others, had noted my presence, there would be no need for a sense of shame. Besides, one of the others had also failed to rise but in doing so, he had seen the events unfold from his bunk, with the added luxury of a small tinted window no bigger than a tablet's screen. He likens the pane to a CCTV monitor, and places two figures — one familiar — gesticulating in the filtered rectangle. I take his information on board and convert it into the dreamlike images of the imagination.

Morning arrives uninterrupted, the alarm switched off with the lethargic swipe of a thumb, and I repeat the midnight act: opening the curtains, craning my neck, this time greeted only by the darkness of the aisle, empty other than a single, marooned sock. As I return the movement another head pops out of the gap between the two curtains opposite, unveiled in a disproportionate theatre show. I greet the protagonist, noticing that his forehead is punctuated with a gash, a small island of browning blood surrounding the wound.

The cliché becomes a reality: I do not know where I am. Do not know which language I must speak. The vehicle, with its shuttered windows, enhances the confusion of the presumed morning, the natural light unable to penetrate and therefore suggest a rough hour. I must once more shuffle down the aisle of bunks, stooping with arms outstretched checking for any obstruction that the darkness might offer. I am not as efficient as the deep-sea fish my mind conjures, its glowing protrusion perhaps likened to the smart phone I have managed to pull from the bed sheets as my aid; a device also responsible for a more accurate sense of orientation in time (late morning). The window shutters are finally lifted to display another framed postcard: a desolate cracked road, flanked by scrubland. Just like the loading compound some weeks ago, the scene offers up its limited props and I begin to scan them for further orientation but, in doing so, another biological filter is revealed: my glasses. They remained in the small netted pocket above the bunk upstairs, and I would be unable to see properly without them. This lack of physical clarity is made all the more clear, mentally, when I spot a van parked across the tarmac in the distance. I am unable to decipher the coloured markings of its surface, although I know from the rough outlines of this buzzing arrangement, that it would give me evidence, some kind of text that would no doubt reveal the unknown details of my location. With my eyes still stuck in the netted pocket above and a distinct lack of enthusiasm for movement, I reach for the glowing protrusion of the phone once more, lifting the lens and zooming with the small spread of thumb and forefinger. I take the photograph, the image announced by the false sound of a non-existent shutter.

'moo-chasse gra-th-ias'

I pronounce the words slowly and poorly in my head.

xii

There is a box of dogs. But at first I
do not know that it is a box of dogs.
I simply think it is a trailer, perhaps
containing surplus goods, or the bikes
of the car's owners. My realisation is
only prompted by the appearance of a
woman from out of the roadside hotel's
three-star doorway. She walks towards
another parked car, before proceeding
to speak tenderly to one of the rear
windows in a language I can't translate.
The action appears understandably
odd, somewhat disconcerting, until I
see a majestic creature rise from the
back seat, pressing its nose against
the pane before she releases the
door's latch to continue her tenderness.
Suddenly, noise erupts from across the
car park: a series of yelps, bumps and
crashes sounding from the small box-
like trailer no more than thirty feet away.
It startles us both. Audibly, it becomes
easy to note a number of animals
inside, and I'm immediately impressed
by the abilities of their scent, so quick to
act upon the potential fulfillment of their
carnal desires — even without sight.
The woman and I stare over the tarmac,
gazing at the hidden bodies inside. I
begin to worry about the size of the
box, begin to worry about the number
of dogs. Perhaps she does too. Either
way, we are bonded in this moment,
only interrupted when a man, presumed
to be her husband, appears from
behind the hotel building, he has a thick
moustache and drags nonchalantly on
a cigarette.

Tension flows through my body.
I am unsociable, at a distance from
conversations I am proximate to.
I question the cause, question its
appearance at this particular moment.
Is it a lack of sleep? An expected
sense of exhaustion after the vehicle's
journey across numerous borders. Or
was it simply chemically induced, the
over-stimulation of two strong cups of
coffee that I almost certainly drank for
the ritual rather than the taste. I probe
deeper still, perhaps it was in fact a
bodily response to my projection of an
unknown future, moments when I would
imagine myself in a stable and happy
relationship. I mention this now, as the
most recent attempt to achieve this view
had crumbled, and she was from this
very location. She was geographically
associated, dissolved into the street
signs above my head, interspersed
in the words uttered in the cafes and
bars I had floated through. It would
be impossible to achieve the ability to
instantly forget, but I wished I could,
so I could simply enjoy the flattened
face of the city for what it was, ignoring
these redemptive call-backs. Maybe
sleep became the only solution
available to me, a cheap, limited version
of forgetting. I would first have to find
my way back to the vehicle, which
would involve navigating a series of
foreign midnight streets to find its
temporary housing: an underground
car-park hidden underneath the city's
grand palace.

I found its grandeur relatively easily,
but struggled to find the car-park's
entrance, idly wandering amongst
the well-kept hedges and statues
before noticing the glowing staircase
that descended to a lift shaft. I felt
some relief as I sank into the concrete
underbelly, as if cleansed in the acid
yellow of tungsten bulbs: this was a
space designated for transit, the transit
of both traffic and dreams. The vehicle
is accessed by an electronic panel,
and the code had become repetitively
etched into the muscle memory of my
fingers. So much so that I was barely
conscious of it, the body's familiarity
masking the action, as if an alien hand
conducted the duty. This time, though,
I'm surprised, and I'm pulled back into
presence. The usual bleeps of the code
panel do not sound. The door does not
make its hissing hydraulic swing. I stand
alone in the yellow hue pondering my
options. The battery could be flat, which
would mean my forgetting would have
to wait (she appears once again).
I hasten my decision to phone the
driver. I had no choice but to wake
him, and he was not the sort of man to
appreciate being summoned from his
own dreams.

My mind, and therefore my eyes,
scan the architecture for evidence.
Searching its details for remnants of
the events that were so well publicised.
The theatre's name is projected
from an illuminated sign through the
vehicle's rain-flecked window pane.
Its linguistic form is overpowered,
the shape and semantics of the word
obscured by the traumatic weight of
its association. A portal to despair.
It is unsettling how quickly the mind
attempts to grapple with this mess of
historical information, it slows like a
car breaking at a crash site, the human
desire for understanding creating
a memorial tailback. I am forced to
recall the incomplete images of the
news broadcasts, superimposing it
onto the experience of the present,
the perspective of my gaze perhaps
mimicking the very position of the
cameras. Upon entry to the building, my
eyes skip across the balconies, through
the painted murals of the walls and onto
the parquet maze of the dance floor.
It is an interior quest, searching for a
physical mark that could offer some
tangible understanding in absolute
devastation. The urge is unavoidable,
but to verbalise the private act would
be insensitive. The reality is that there
are no visible traces. There is simply
no access.

November
John Henry Newton

written on the road between 29/10 and 02/12, 2018, designed by åbäke, editing assisted by Barnie Page, first published by Dent-De-Leone 2019 in an edition of 111, signed and numbered, printed on the road in Amsterdam (cover screenprinted at AGALAB with David Pons on Amsterdam city maps and Mondriaan fund leaflets), London (vii, viii, ix and x printed on an HP Color LaserPrinter with Jim Bicknell-Knight at Ryan Gander's studio), Boulogne-sur-Mer (v, vi, xi and xii printed on a Konika Minolta BizhubC308 with Frédérique Mascot at Maison des Enfants de la Côte d'Opale), Amman (iii, iv, xiii and xiv on 80gsm Laser Printed with Noura Salem at MMAG foundation and photocopied on Ricoh Aticio mp c4000 for JD 6.9 [£7.53]) and Kasterlee (i, ii, xv and xvi on 80gsm Risographed with David Pons at Frans Masereel Centrum).

Thanks to: Freeman Abayasekera, Dan Anthony, Jon Beavis, Mark Bent, Lucy Bent, Jim Bicknell-Knight, Mark Bowen, Rosie Bright, Gabi Davies, Mags Daly, Adam Devonshire, Lauren Doughty, Chris Fullard, Ryan Gander, Katherine Gardner, Luca George, Adriënne Groen, Johnny Healey, Bob Higson, Sue Higson, Amy Houmøller, Ann-Marie James, Joshua Jarman, Alexandre Khondji, Lee Kiernan, Jack Looker, Phil Mayer, Paul Melbourne, Lindsay Melbourne, Jeremy Millar, Thomas Needham, Veronika Neukirch, Kathy Newton, David Newton, Phil Newton, Liam Sexton, Name Surname, Leonie Sinden, Joseph Talbot, James Tones, Viviana Troya, Alex Wealands, Jonathan P Watts.

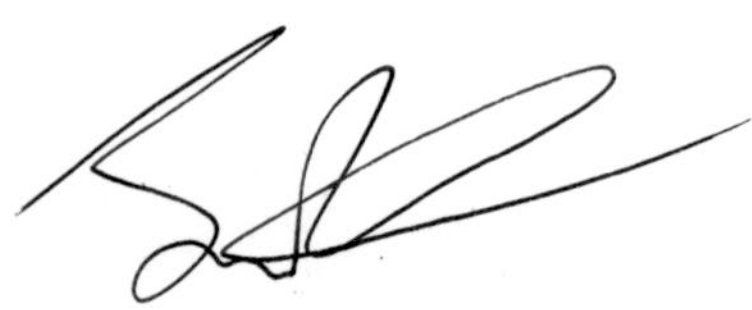

ISBN 978-1-907908-53-8

074 / 111

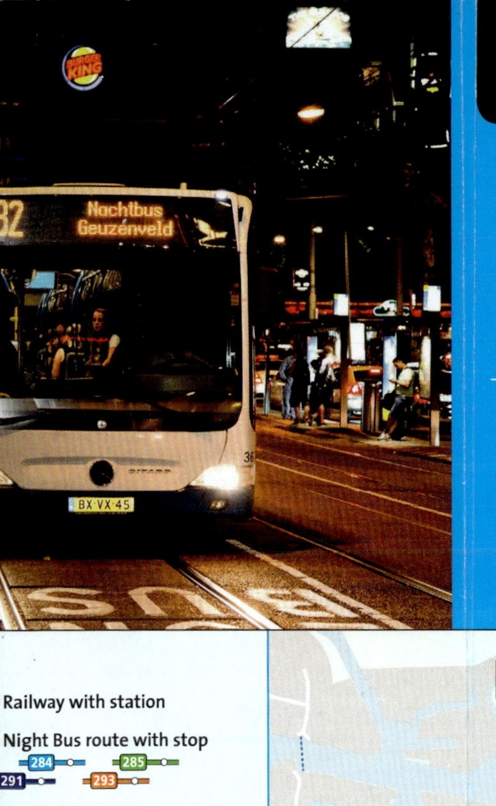

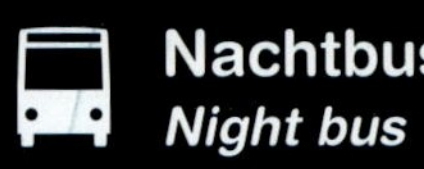

Nachtbus
Night bus

Naast de speciale GVB nachtbus reisproducten zijn ook geldig in
GVB dagkaart (1 t/m 7 dagen), Amsterdam Travel Ticket, Amsterda
Holland Travel Ticket en de abonnementen: GVB Only, GVB Zone
in de keuzezone(s)), OV-jaarabonnement en het Netabonnement.

*Besides the special night bus travel products are also valid on th
GVB day ticket (1-7 days), Amsterdam Travel Ticket, Amsterdam
Travel Ticket and the season tickets: GVB Only, GVB Zone and Ra
zone(s) only), OV annual ticket (for all public transport in the Neth*

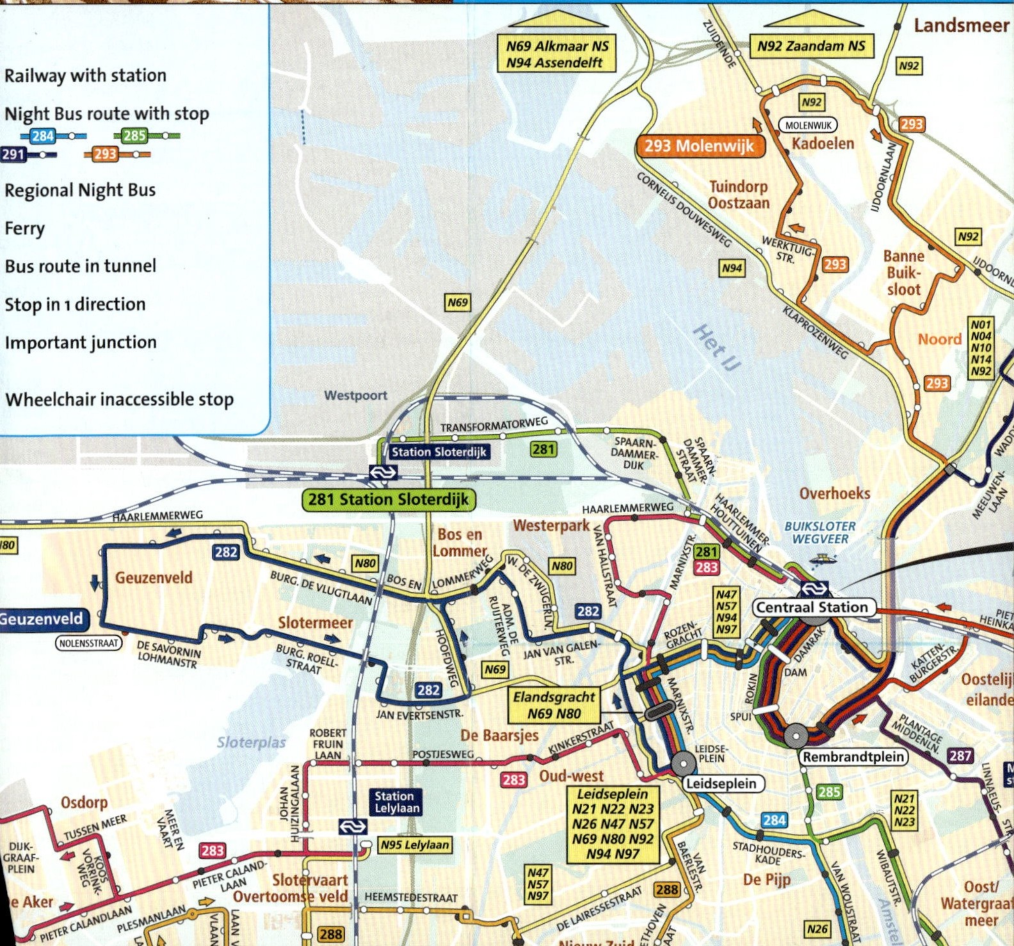

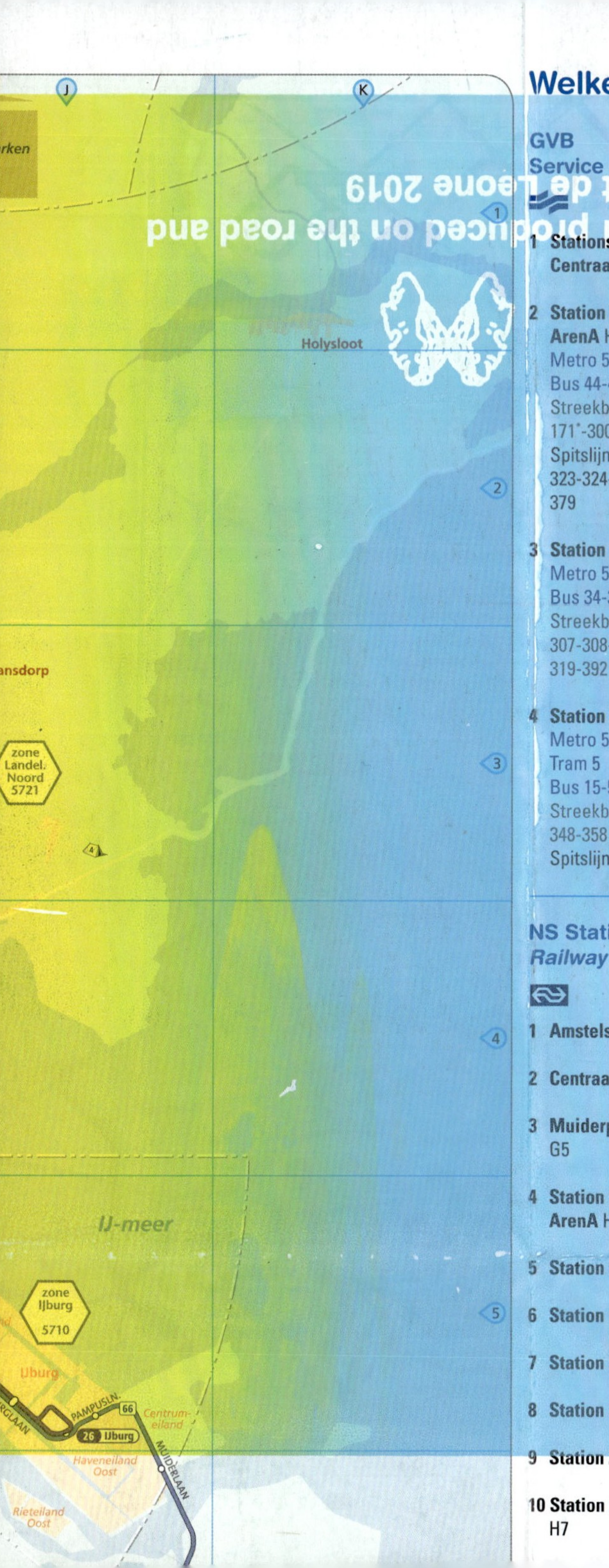

Welke lijn? / *Which line?*

GVB
Service & Tickets

1 Stationsplein
Centraal Station F4

2 Station Bijlmer
ArenA H8
Metro 50-54
Bus 44-47-49*-66
Streekbus 120-126-
171*-300-328-356-376*
Spitslijn 202-255-271-
323-324-375-377-378-
379

3 Station Noord G2
Metro 52
Bus 34-36*-37-38
Streekbus 301*-304-
307-308-312-315-
319-392

4 Station Zuid E6
Metro 50-51-52
Tram 5
Bus 15-55-62-65
Streekbus 341-346-
348-358
Spitslijn 242

NS Stations
Railway stations

1 Amstelstation G6

2 Centraal Station F4

3 Muiderpoortstation
G5

4 Station Bijlmer
ArenA H8

5 Station Diemen I6

6 Station Lelylaan D5

7 Station RAI F6

8 Station Sloterdijk D3

9 Station Zuid E6

10 Station Duivendrecht
H7

Musea / *Museums*

1 Amsterdam Museum
F4
Metro 52
Tram 2-4-11*-12-14-24

2 Anne Frankhuis F4
Tram 13-17

4 Joods Historisch
Museum F4
Metro 51-53-54
Tram 14

5 Rembrandthuis F4
Metro 51-53-54
Tram 14

6 Rijksmuseum F5
Tram 1-2-3-5-7-12-19
Streekbus 347-357-
397

7 Scheepvaartmuseum
G4
Bus 22-48

8 Stedelijk Museum F5
Tram 2-3-5-12
Streekbus 347-357-
397

9 Tropenmuseum G5
Tram 7-14-19

10 Van Gogh Museum F5
Tram 2-3-5-12
Streekbus 347-357-
397

11 Verzetsmuseum G4
Tram 14

12 NEMO G4
Bus 22-48

14 Bijbels Museum F4
Tram 2-11*-12

15 Artis/Planetarium/
Micropia G4
Tram 14

16 Allard Pierson
Museum F4
Metro 52
Tram 4-14-24

Medis
instell
Medic
Institu

H

1 Amst
AMC
Kinde
AMC
Metro
Bus 4
Stree

Psyc
Centr
Stree

2 Zieke
land
Bus 5
Stree
551

3 Anton
hoek
Tram
Bus 1
Stree

4 Sanq
zienin
Tram
Bus 1
Stree

5 Boerh
Centr
Tram
Bus 6

6 Bover
huis G
Bus 3-
Stree

7 OLVG
Metro
Tram
Bus 3

8 READ
Tram

9 OLVG
Metro
Tram

12 Ar
m

GVB

us:
l Ticket,
ord Zone (alleen

cket, Holland
one (in selected
et season ticket.

281 **(Station Sloterdijk)**: Centraal Station - Station Sloterdijk (Carrascoplein) v.v.
282 **(Geuzenveld)**: Centraal Station - Leidseplein - Marcantiplaza/Centrale markthallen - Geuzenveld - Centraal Station
283 **(Osdorp De Aker)**: Centraal Station - Leidseplein - Station Lelylaan - Osdorp De Aker - Centraal Station
284 **(Amstelveen Busstation)**: Centraal Station - Leidseplein - Station RAI - Amstelveen Busstation
285 **(Gein)**: Centraal Station - Rembrandtplein - Amstelstation - Station Bijlmer ArenA - Gaasperplas - Centraal Station
287 **(Bijlmermeer)**: Centraal Station - Rembrandtplein - Station Diemen - Station Diemen Zuid - Station Bijlmer ArenA - Centraal Station
288 **(Nieuw Sloten)**: Centraal Station - Leidseplein - Nieuw Sloten - Centraal Station
289 **(IJburg)**: Centraal Station - Rembrandtplein - Indische Buurt - IJburg - Centraal Station
291 **(Nieuwendam)**: Centraal Station - Rembrandtplein - Camping Vliegenbos - Nieuwendam - Centraal Station
293 **(Molenwijk)**: Centraal Station - Rembrandtplein - Molenwijk - Banne Buiksloot - Centraal Station

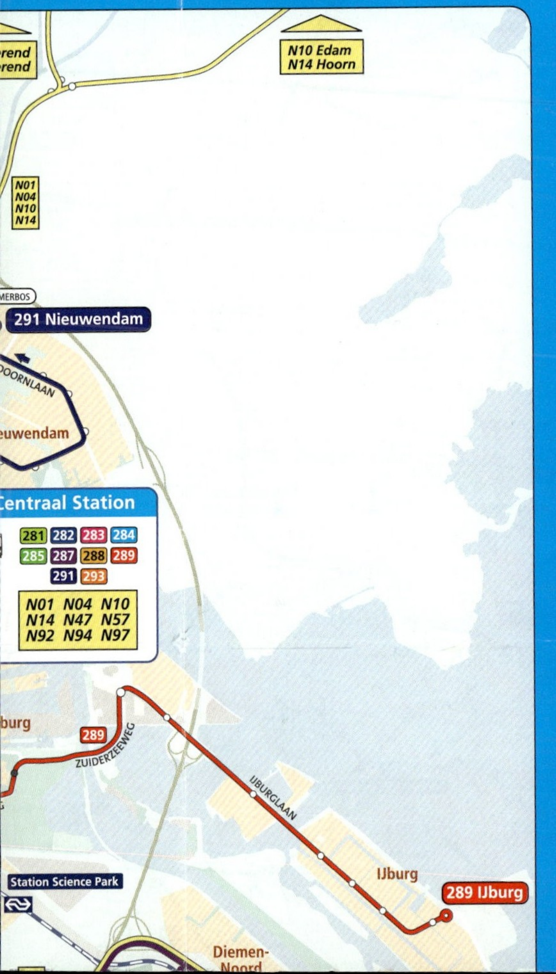

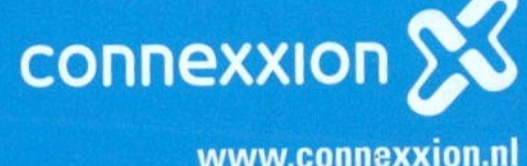

N30 Station Bijlmer ArenA - Amstelveen - Schiphol/ Airport Plaza - Hoofddorp- Haarlem
N47 Uithoorn - Centraal Station
N57 Aalsmeer - Amstelveen - Centraal Station
N69 Elandsgracht - Leidseplein - Krommenie Station - Limmen - Heiloo - Alkmaar
N80 Leidseplein - Haarlem - IJmuiden
N92 Leidseplein - Centraal Station - Landsmeer - Oost zaan - Zaandam Station
N94 Leidseplein - Centraal Station - Zaandam Station - Assendelft NS - Westzaan
N95 Amsterdam Lelylaan - Schiphol Airport
N97 Nieuw Vennep - Schiphol Airport - Centraal Station

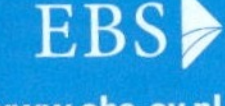

N01 Centraal Station - Watergang - Ilpendam - Purmerend
N04 Centraal Station - Watergang - Ilpendam - Purmerend
N10 Centraal Station - Broek in Waterland - Monnickendam - Katwoude - Volendam - Edam
N14 Centraal Station - Broek in Waterland - Monnickendam - Hoorn Station

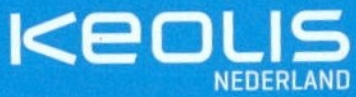

N21 Leidseplein – Almere Buiten
N22 Leidseplein – Almere Buiten

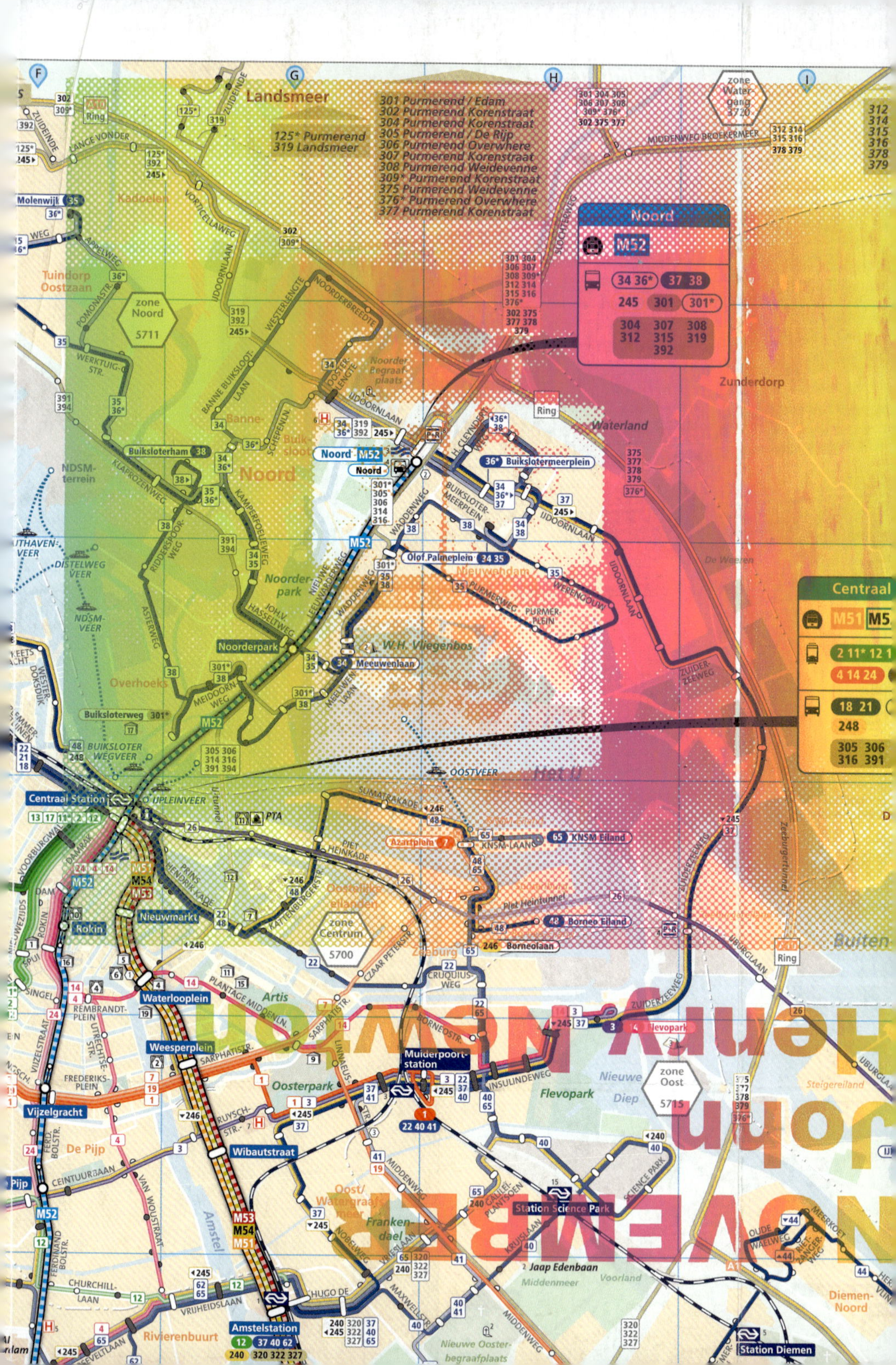

NOVEMBER
John
Henry Newton